Heryin Books
1033 E. Main St., #202, Alhambra, CA 91801
Printed in Taiwan All rights reserved.
www.heryin.com

Library of Congress Cataloging-in-Publication Data
Yang, Huan, 1930-1954.
Homes / written by Yang-Huan ; illustrated by Hsiao-yen Huang.
-- 1st ed.   p. cm.
Summary: The dwellings of different animals and insects are
portrayed in a poem, reminding children of the meaning of home.
I. Huang, Hsiao-yen, 1965- II. Title.
PL2922.H66 2005   895.1'152--dc22   2005013421
ISBN 0-9762056-3-7

Homes

Yang-Huan / Hsiao-yen Huang

 Books

Alhambra, California

Leaves are cribs for tiny caterpillars.

Flowers are slumbering beds
for butterflies.

All singing birds
have cozy nests.

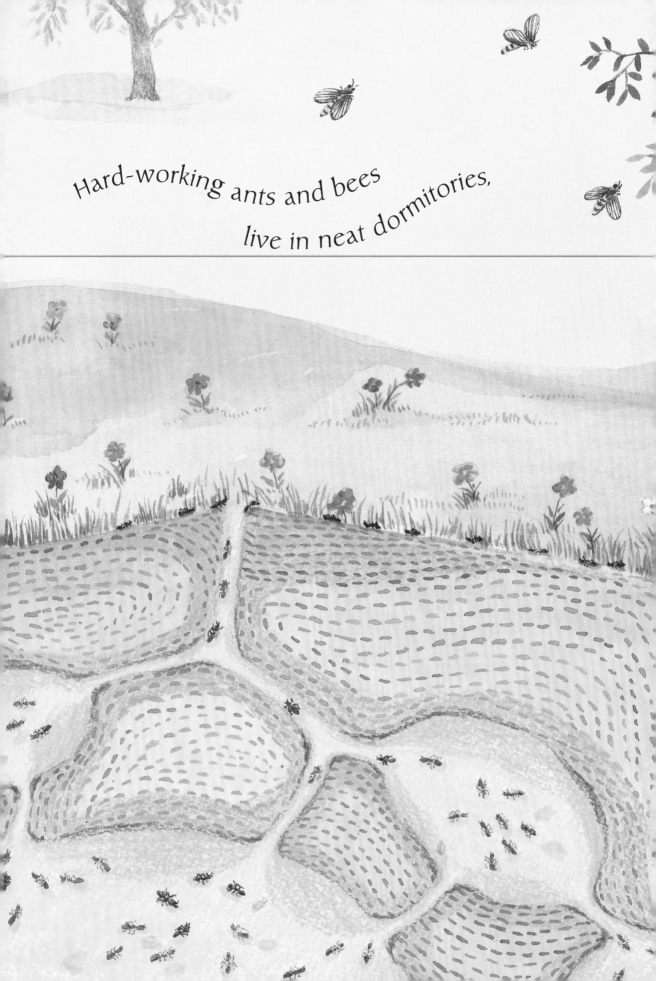

Hard-working ants and bees
live in neat dormitories,

Crab's and fish's homes are in blue creeks.

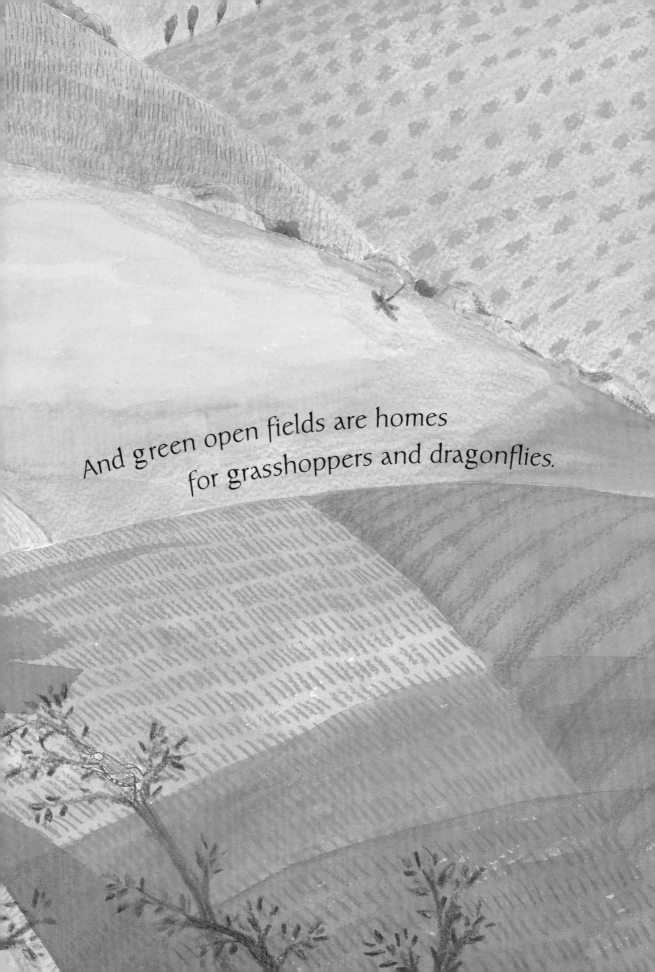

And green open fields are homes
for grasshoppers and dragonflies.

Poor wind has no home,

Running east and west

with no place to rest.

Traveling clouds have no home.

They are so anxious that their tears flow whenever the sky darkens.

The little boys and girls are the luckiest!
Their parents get their homes ready when they are born,
So they can grow up safe and sound in their homes.